CLEANING UP THE EARTH

Precious McKenzie

ROURKE PUBLISHING

www.rourkepublishing.com

www.rourkepublishing.com

PHOTO CREDITS: Cover: © Danny Hooks, Robert Bush; Title Page: © Valerie Matthews; Page 4, 12: © Ralph125; Page 5: © Patrick Herrera; Page 6: © Bart Coenders; Page 7: © Fabio Filzi; Page 9: © mbbirdy; Page 10: © Carmen Martínez Banús; Page 11: © Catherine Yeulet; Page 13: © mark wragg; Page 14: © NoDerog; Page 15: © fabphoto; Page 16: © Bryan Brayley-Willmetts; Page 17: © ranplett; Page 18: © Abel Mitja Varela; Page 19: © kristian sekulic; Page 21: © Robert Churchill; Page 22: © Jani Bryson;

Edited by Meg Greve

Cover and Interior design by Tara Raymo

Library of Congress Cataloging-in-Publication Data

McKenzie, Precious
 Cleaning Up the Earth / Precious McKenzie.
     p. cm. -- (Green Earth Science Discovery Library)
 Includes bibliographical references and index.
 ISBN 978-1-61741-768-9 (hard cover) (alk. paper)
 ISBN 978-1-61741-970-6 (soft cover)
 Library of Congress Control Number: 2011924814

Rourke Publishing
Printed in the United States of America, North Mankato, Minnesota
060711
060711CL

RouRke PublishinG

www.rourkepublishing.com - rourke@rourkepublishing.com
Post Office Box 643328 Vero Beach, Florida 32964

Table of Contents

Pollution

Pollution happens when people leave trash or **chemicals** in the air, soil, or water.

Fumes from factories and cars make it hard for people to breathe.

Garbage in oceans and rivers kills fish and aquatic plants.

Scientists collect water and soil samples to measure the amount of pollution.

Global Warming

Many **environmentalists** think pollution causes global warming. Global warming happens when the Earth's temperature rises because greenhouse gases become trapped in the Earth's **atmosphere**.

Help Clean Up!

You and your family can help in many ways.

Plant trees and flowers to help combat air pollution.

Ride your bicycle or walk instead of riding in a car to reduce the amount of **carbon dioxide** in the air.

Recycle your trash to reduce the amount of waste in **landfills**.

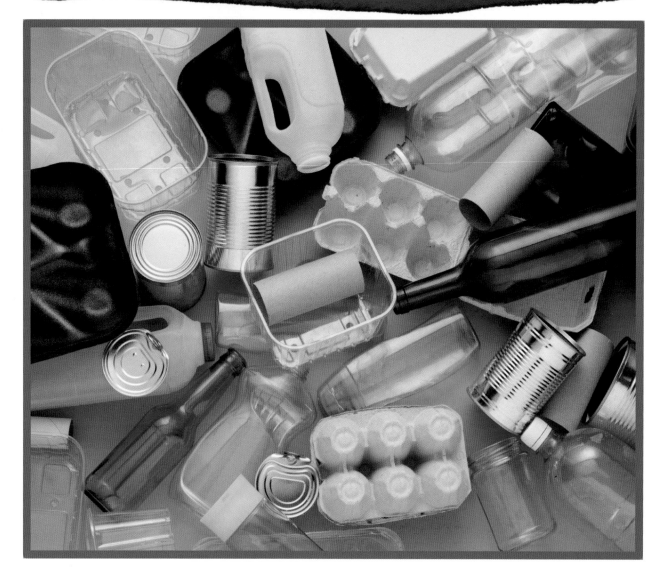

You can recycle plastic, glass, paper, and metal.

Take batteries, paints, oils, and medical supplies to special disposal sites.

Workers make sure that this toxic waste is disposed of properly so that nothing seeps into the **groundwater** supply.

Do not litter. Throw your trash in garbage cans, not on the ground or in the ocean.

Talk to your friends. Tell them how they can help clean up our world.

What Can You Do?

Write to your local and national politicians.

Tell them you want laws that stop pollution.

Laws can protect the environment.

You can also write to local and national businesses. Ask them to recycle and cut down on harmful pollution.

Our Earth is our beautiful home. We must take care of it so that we all have a safe, clean place to live.

Support businesses that recycle.

Try This

You don't have to wait until you are an adult to make the Earth a better place to live. Try these simple ideas to take care of our planet.

1. Turn off and unplug all of your electronic toys when you are not using them.
2. Dress in warmer clothes in the winter and keep the heat turned down.
3. Plant a tree.
4. Ride a bike, walk, or skateboard instead of riding in a car.
5. Organize your friends and neighbors to help clean up a park or beach near you.

Glossary

atmosphere (AT-muhss-fihr): different kinds of gases that surround a planet

carbon dioxide (KAR-buhn dye-OK-side): a gas with no color or smell that people and animals breathe out

chemicals (KEM-uh-kuhls): substances that are used in science and manufacturing that can be harmful when not used carefully

environmentalists (en-VYE-ruhn-ment-uhl-ists): people who study the Earth's environment, especially pollution

groundwater (GROUND-waw-tur): water found under the Earth's surface

landfills (LAND-fils): huge places where garbage trucks dump trash

Index

Websites

www.pbskids.org/shareastory/stories/64/index.html

www.clean-air-kids.org.uk/globalwarming.html

www.kidsforsavingearth.org/index.html

About the Author

Precious McKenzie lives in Florida with her husband, three children, and two dogs. She writes books for children and teaches English at the University of South Florida. In her free time, she enjoys being outside.